Puppies in 3-D

Puppies in 3-D
Copyright © 2010 GENKOSHA Co.

First Japanese edition published in 2010 by
GENKOSHA Co., Tokyo Japan

HarperCollins books may be purchased for educational, business, or sales promotional use. For information, please write: Special Markets Department, HarperCollins*Publishers*, 10 East 53rd Street, New York, NY 10022.

First English edition published in 2011 by:
Harper Design
An Imprint of HarperCollins*Publishers*
10 East 53rd Street
New York, NY 10022
Tel: (212) 207-7000
Fax: (212) 207-7654
harperdesign@harpercollins.com
www.harpercollins.com
Through the rights and production arrangement of Rico Komanoya, ricorico, Tokyo, Japan.

Distributed throughout the world by:
HarperCollins*Publishers*
10 East 53rd Street
New York, NY 10022
Tel: (212) 207-7000
Fax: (212) 207-7654

Photographs: Yoneo Morita (noa noa)
Photography assistants: Naomi Shirakawa, Yoshimi Toyoda
Illustration: Tsuyuko Tamai
Editorial cooperation: Little Dog (Moriya), Yuriko Sugiyama, Akikne Hirasaka, Kenji Kitami, Akira Hiba, Yoichi Yonemura, Noboru Yoshida, Hiroyuki Hayashi, Noriko Hirayama, Naohisa Yoshifuji, Kenji Kaneko, Takahiro Yamagishi, Gyoko Torai, Mio Honda, Minako Sakuma, Yoshie Fukatani, Midori Takeda, Mari Akimoto, Kyoko Suzuki, Minoru Yamazaki, Kaoru Sato, Yumiko Muramatsu, Reiko Nagao, and Natsumi Kuwabara
English translation: Kayoko Kimata
English translation/copy-editing: Alma Reyes (ricorico)
Book design and art direction: Makoto Tamaki (Erg), Andrew Pothecary (forbiddencolour)
Editor: Akira Fujii
Chief editor and production: Rico Komanoya (ricorico)

ISBN: 978-0-06-203958-3

Library of Congress Control Number: 2010943221

Printed in China by Everbest Printing Co., Ltd.

First Printing, 2011

Puppies in 3-D

Yoneo Morita

HARPER DESIGN

An Imprint of HarperCollins Publishers

Play with me!

Contents

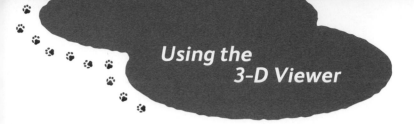

Using the 3-D Viewer

3-D Viewing Technique

Pictures with the **3-D** mark can be viewed three-dimensionally using the 3-D viewer. The distance between the 3-D viewer and the pictures should be around 7.5-12 inches; however, this varies per person. If you are not able to see the pictures in 3-D, try to adjust the distance between the viewer and the pictures while keeping the 3-D viewer close to your face. For pages with three images next to each other, the center image is viewed in 3-D. Focus on the center image and adjust the distance between the viewer and the picture. You can find the appropriate focal point and 3-D effect that suits you.

Using the 3-D viewer may cause eye fatigue. Avoid using it for long hours.

Viewing Puppies in 3-D

Viewing puppies in 3-D, not in plane dimension, is the best way to experience these charming photographs. With this three-dimensional effect, the puppies look as though they are sitting in the palm of your hand.

Images with the **3-D** mark can give you an enriched sense of the dogs' fur and the shape of their noses and tails as well as the movement of their tongues and ears in detail. *Puppies in 3-D* delivers the wonderful characteristics of puppies in a much more real and vivid way.

Poodle

Poodle

🐾 Origin

The Poodle is popular all around the world, especially in France, where it is called the French Poodle. Its ancestors are believed to be dogs that were very good at hunting by the coastal waters of Germany; hence, the dog's name was adapted from *pudel*, a German term meaning "to move forward with the rising splash of water."

🐾 Physical Appearance

The Poodle's physical appearance is well balanced and elegant. It has moderately strong muscles. Its eyes are almond-shaped, and its lips are tight. Its hair color varies from being black, white, and brown to apricot. Some Poodles have single-colored hair, while others are shaded in varying colors.
   Since the Poodle was originally a waterfowl retriever, the hair around its legs is trimmed so that it can move about easily in the water. Alternately, the fur around its stomach may be retained so as to protect its hearts and lungs. This elegant trimming style has become known as the "Poodle cut."

🐾 Character

The Poodle is a very clever dog. It is easily trained and obedient, and can be taught all manner of things. It is an active dog and likes to take walks. It also likes to play, especially with its master. When trained patiently, it can also learn tricks.

Such cute paws!

*My neck juts out when
I'm surprised.*

Poodle

Rolling...relaxing...over and over again...

Oops... *I heard a sound.*

Poodle

I'm so fluffy!

15

Poodle

I can hardly
squeeze inside
this cup!

Uh-oh...I think
I lost my way...

Poodle

Shake my paws!

That's funny! Ha! Ha! Ha!

Poodle

French Bulldog

 # French Bulldog

Origin

During the 1880s, certain dogs were raised and crossbred by enthusiastic breeders from downtown Paris, France. Eventually, they were hybridized with bulldogs, terriers, and pugs imported from England. These dogs were primarily used to rid Paris's central market of mice. Later, these dogs were accepted by the Parisians for their unique appearance, and were taken into high society and the world of artists.

Physical Appearance

The French Bulldog has a rough physical appearance with sturdy muscles and a firm bone structure. It has a smashed-up looking face and a pug nose. Its ears look like the wings of a bat, and it has deep facial wrinkles. The tail is short, and the body is covered with glossy and comparatively short and coarse hair. The nose, eyes, and eyelids are usually dark in color.

Character

The French Bulldog is an active dog with a well-defined character. It is very sociable and likes to play, partake in sports, and do other types of exercise. It is very strong and, unlike the English Bulldog, moves quickly. It seldom barks, but may snore a bit. It is affectionate with its master and with children. Unfortunately, it can sometimes act a bit spoiled, but this characteristic is surprisingly endearing.

The French Bulldog is a good watchdog. It is bred domestically, and likes to be taken out for walks in the open air.

French Bulldog

French Bulldog

Chihuahua

Chihuahua

Origin

The origin of the Chihuahua's name comes from Chihuahua State, the biggest of the thirty-one states in Mexico. The Chihuahua was originally considered to be a wild dog, but was domesticated by the Indios during the period of the Toltec Civilization around the ninth century. It was imported from Mexico to America, and since then, its popularity—and appearance—has spread all over the world.

Physical Appearance

The Chihuahua is the smallest dog in the world. Its bone structure is slender, making its body very flexible. The head is round, and is called an apple head because the back of the head looks like an apple when it is raised. It also has bright, round, and big eyes. The color of its pupils varies from being black to being brightly colored. The fur may be either smooth and short or long. The hair color ranges from chocolate, blue, black, or red, to other variations.

Character

The Chihuahua is a very loyal dog that easily adapts to training. If it is appropriately trained, it shows deep affections toward its master. It is very quick, cautious, active, and brave. Its appearance may not show it, but it asserts itself boldly, even toward larger dogs. The Chihuahua enjoys taking sunbaths and prefers to exercise indoors rather than outside.

Unmindful look

Chihuahua

Chihuahua

I love running!

Uh... *Is there something on my butt?*

Chihuahua

Zzz...zzz...

Chihuahua

Uh-oh...I'm falling...!

Chihuahua

Beautiful flowers!

Dachshund

Dachshund

🐾 Origin

The Dachshund is the result of crossbreeding middle-sized pinschers with the Jura Hound from Germany and Austria during the Middle Ages. The Dachshund was raised to flush out badgers and other burrow-dwelling animals. The legs are short not only for this purpose, but also to facilitate hunting smaller prey, such as rabbits.

🐾 Physical Appearance

The Dachshund has short legs, a long torso, and a long and narrow face. It is a very muscular dog, which is surprising for its tiny build. It has three types of hair: smooth, glossy, and short; wiry, rough, and curly; and wavy, soft, and long. The hair color ranges from being red, black, cream, yellow, or chocolate, to other variations.

🐾 Character

The Dachshund is very friendly and affectionate to humans. It is generally a calm dog, though it can act nervously at times. It is rarely aggressive. It moves quickly, and is a great watchdog. Because it is both obedient and cheerful—and adorable to boot—it is easily favored as a pet. It also has great stamina for activity and, therefore, prefers to exercise outdoors.

Kick!

What are you doing?

Dachshund

"I've been working on the railroad..."

That's dangerous!

The Dachshund's Growing Years

22 days old

1 month and 20 days old

Mother Dachshund and babies

3 months and 7 days old

8 days old

5 and a half months old

3-D

My imitation of a seal.

45

Dachshund

Can you see this?

Pomeranian

Pomeranian

Origin

The Pomeranian was bred as a sheep dog in the Pomerania region of Eastern Europe. Because of its miniature size, it was highly favored in England during the eighteenth century. In fact, it was Queen Victoria's favorite type of dog. Since the middle of the nineteenth century, miniature-sized dogs—like the Samoyed sheepdog, for example—have become very popular. The Pomeranian is descended from the Spitz type dog. Considered a member of the toy dog breed, the Pomeranian doesn't know its own size and is very protective of its master.

Physical Appearance

The Pomeranian has soft, long, and abundantly beautiful hair, a round and small forehead, and a slim appearance, which are also the characteristics of the Spitz family dog type, known for its slender legs. The small ears are triangular-shaped and stand erect. The tail is long, with its base extending from the hips, and rolls up to the center of the back. When the Pomeranian shakes its body, the tail moves to show off its long, decorative fur.

   It has colorful hair, ranging in tones from black, brown, chocolate, red, orange, and cream to white. It may also have a mixture of a single color or two colors.

Character

The Pomeranian is cautious, active, loyal, and can be very accommodating. It is also obedient, cheerful, clever, and very affectionate. It is not a coward nor offensive, and is, therefore, easily favored by dog masters. It also has a good memory, which makes it easily trainable as a capable watchdog. It often barks.

   The knees may be easily dislocated due to their slender bone structure; therefore, it is not advisable to expose the Pomeranian to extreme exercise.

Pomeranian

Papillon

✳ Papillon

🐾 Origin

The Papillon's ancestor is a kind of spaniel from Spain. *Papillon* means "butterfly" in French, and is coined for this type of dog because its ears resemble the shape of butterfly wings. The Papillon is small, and is also called *Epagneul nain*, "inch-high spaniel," or butterfly spaniel.

It was bred in the region of Bologna, Italy, during the period of Louis XIV in the fourteenth century.

🐾 Physical Appearance

The most outstanding characteristic of the Papillon is its big ears. The length of the hair is medium, and it is straight and soft. The Papillon also has decorative hair around the ears, chest, legs, and tail. The hair color is clear against a white background. Some dogs' ears may droop; this type of Papillon is called *Phalène*. The eyes are big and dark, and the nose is black. It is a very elegant dog, slender and small, and is typical of the Toy Spaniel.

🐾 Character

The Papillon is active and moves quickly. It is intelligent and strong, and may either be bold and brave, or sensitive and spoiled. It is sensitive to the master's behavior and can be a very obedient domestic dog if trained well. One quirk: It may show some stress by barking for no reason. Alternately, it can also be shy.

Papillon

*This branch has
no taste.*

Papillon

Yorkshire Terrier

Yorkshire Terrier

🐾 *Origin*

The Yorkshire Terrier was bred as a working dog that hunted mice in factories in Yorkshire, England, during the mid-nineteenth century. In 1862, the breed was named Broken Haired Scotch, but this name was later changed to Yorkshire Terrier.

Today, this dog is most commonly known as Yorkie. Toward the end of the nineteenth century, the Yorkshire Terrier became a very popular pet among the high society of noble ladies.

🐾 *Physical Appearance*

Traditionally, the Yorkie hair should be glossy, fine, straight, and silky. The coat is grown-out long and parted down the middle of the back so it hangs down in a straight fashion. Its colorful coat requires much care to maintain its beauty and high-gloss tone. The Yorkie has a charming look and a firm physique. It is a small dog with a dignified appearance and manner.

🐾 *Character*

The Yorkshire Terrier is very cautious and smart. It has a strong competitive spirit, and is active and vigorous. Very loyal to its master, it is also calm and brave. Fiercely territorial, it makes a fine watchdog and, in general, is a great pet.

Yorkshire Terrier

The Yorkshire Terrier's Growing Years

4 and a half months old

2 months old

1 and a half years old

It's fun to see the Yorkshire Terrier's fur color change in time. The three puppies shown above are of the same dog, and show their fur color change from dark during the infant age, to light during the older years. It is said that the fur color changes twelve times in one lifetime. The Yorkshire Terrier shown on the left shows its long and shaggy fur, which is said to resemble a curtain of glittering jewelry.

Yorkshire Terrier

Japanese Shiba

Japanese Shiba

🐾 Origin

The Japanese Shiba is the oldest dog in Japan, and has been the country's native dog since ancient times. *Shiba* means "a small thing" or in this context, a small dog, though the origin of the dog's name comes from its hair color, which resembles that of a cut lawn. It most commonly lived in the mountain regions along the Japan Sea, and was used for hunting small animals and birds. It was crossbred with English dogs, making the genuine Japanese Shiba quite rare to find.

The Japanese Shiba normally does not bark for any reason, and is highly regarded as a domestic dog. It is especially beloved in America.

🐾 Physical Appearance

While relatively small, the Japanese Shiba has a strong bone structure and well-developed muscles. Its movements are alert, agile, and quick. It has short and stiff outer and soft down hair. The hair color ranges from being red, gray, and reddish black, to black brown, and other variations. It also has white hair around the cheeks, chest, and stomach. During the change of seasons, the hair may shed a lot. Temperamentally, the Japanese Shiba has a simple charm, which is further complemented by its quiet beauty.

🐾 Character

The Japanese Shiba is a loyal dog and is very obedient. It is active and clever, and has a keen sense for being extremely cautious. Hence, it is a very good watchdog. One distinguishing characteristic of the breed is the so-called "shiba-scream." When sufficiently perturbed, the dog will emit a high-pitched scream. On occasion, a similar sound may accompany moments of great joy.

My cute nose

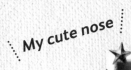

My paws...

Japanese Shiba

**Look at my
standing whiskers.**

Japanese Shiba

I love rolling on the floor!

Japanese Shiba

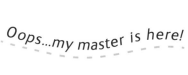
Oops...my master is here!

74

Italian Greyhound

Italian Greyhound

Origin

The Italian Greyhound is an ancient breed of hounds that hunts by speed and sight. A greyhound was said to be discovered in the lava during the eruption of Mt. Vesuvius in Pompeii, Italy, in 79 AD. Thereafter, it became very popular among the noblemen during the Renaissance period. During the 1700s, King Frederick II of Prussia set off to war with an Italian Greyhound. He loved this dog so much that he was buried with it in his graveyard, next to his palace in Potsdam, Germany.

Physical Appearance

The Italian Greyhound has a slender body with a deep, tucked-up abdomen. The head is long and narrow; the ears are small and folded back; the eyes are dark and medium-sized; and the neck is long and tapered. It has a variety of coat colors, from gray, red, black, and white to cream.

Character

Being affectionate and kind are the Italian Greyhound's most pleasant characteristics that make it a likeable companion dog. It loves to run and play, and enjoys the company of children. It is also very intelligent and may respond only to the master's voice.

Lick! Such a long tongue, huh?

Italian Greyhound

We can run really fast!

Look to the left,
then look ahead!

Italian Greyhound

Elegant posture...

...but, I get tired.

Jack Russell Terrier

Jack Russell Terrier

Origin

The Jack Russell Terrier is a small terrier known for hunting fox. Its name originates from the name of Reverend John Russell of Devonshire, England, who bred terriers to hunt fox in the mid-to-late 1800s. The terrier has been well preserved as a working dog for over two hundred years.

Physical Appearance

As a working terrier, the Jack Russell Terrier is strong and tough, and has a well-proportioned body. It has clean shoulders, straight legs, and a small chest, which allow it to enter burrows with ease. It has dark, almond-shaped eyes and small, V-shaped ears. The coat may either be smooth or rough, or a combination of both.

Character

The Jack Russell Terrier is known to be highly intelligent, alert, athletic, and brave. It is extremely energetic and can easily be bored if not stimulated regularly. As a hunting dog, it also pursues any creature it encounters.

3-D

Jack Russell Terrier

What are you doing?

This floor is a bit slippery.

Jack Russell Terrier

Italian Greyhound ↘

Pomeranian ↘

↳ Yorkshire Terrier

Papillon ↖

Chihuahua ↘

Puppies

French Bulldog

Jack Russell Terrier

Japanese Shiba

Dachshund

Poodle

Photographer's Profile

Yoneo Morita is well known in Japan for his adorable photographs of puppies and kittens. He uses a technique called *hanadeka* ("big nose"), which is widely employed in Japanese iconography. This technique shrinks the animal's body in relation to its nose. Morita is the author of *Utterly Adorable Cats* and *Utterly Loveable Dogs*. He lives in Japan.